TEENS IN BRAZIL

Teens in Brazil

Brazil

by Caryn Gracey Jones

Content Adviser: Jose Javier Lopez, Ph.D.,
Associate Professor, Department of Geography,
Minnesota State University, Mankato

Reading Adviser: Peggy Ballard, Ph.D.
Department of Educational Studies,
Minnesota State University, Mankato

Compass Point Books ◈ Minneapolis, Minnesota

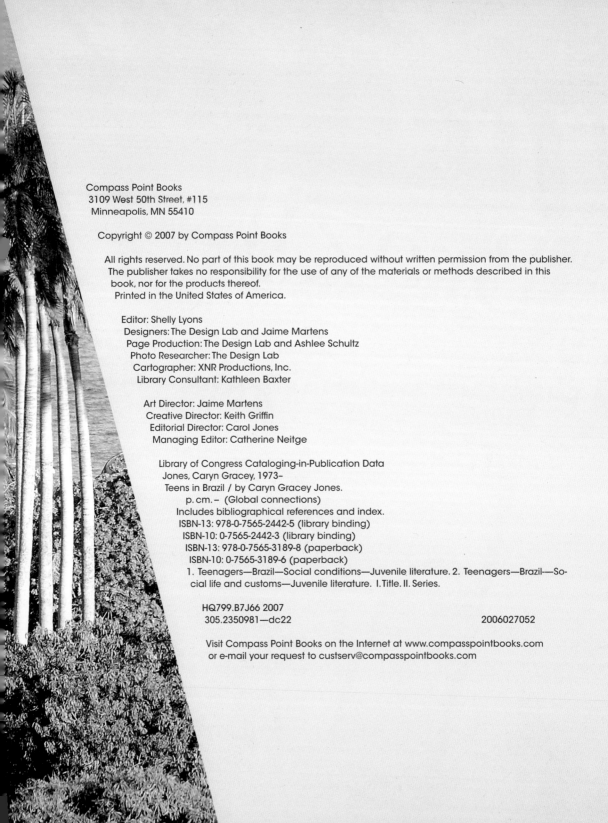

Compass Point Books
3109 West 50th Street, #115
Minneapolis, MN 55410

Editor: Shelly Lyons
Designers: The Design Lab and Jaime Martens
Page Production: The Design Lab and Ashlee Schultz
Photo Researcher: The Design Lab
Cartographer: XNR Productions, Inc.
Library Consultant: Kathleen Baxter

Art Director: Jaime Martens
Creative Director: Keith Griffin
Editorial Director: Carol Jones
Managing Editor: Catherine Neitge

Library of Congress Cataloging-in-Publication Data
Jones, Caryn Gracey, 1973–
Teens in Brazil / by Caryn Gracey Jones.
    p. cm. – (Global connections)
Includes bibliographical references and index.
ISBN-13: 978-0-7565-2442-5 (library binding)
ISBN-10: 0-7565-2442-3 (library binding)
ISBN-13: 978-0-7565-3189-8 (paperback)
ISBN-10: 0-7565-3189-6 (paperback)
1. Teenagers—Brazil—Social conditions—Juvenile literature. 2. Teenagers—Brazil—So-
cial life and customs—Juvenile literature. I. Title. II. Series.

HQ799.B7J66 2007
305.2350981—dc22   2006027052

Visit Compass Point Books on the Internet at www.compasspointbooks.com
or e-mail your request to custserv@compasspointbooks.com

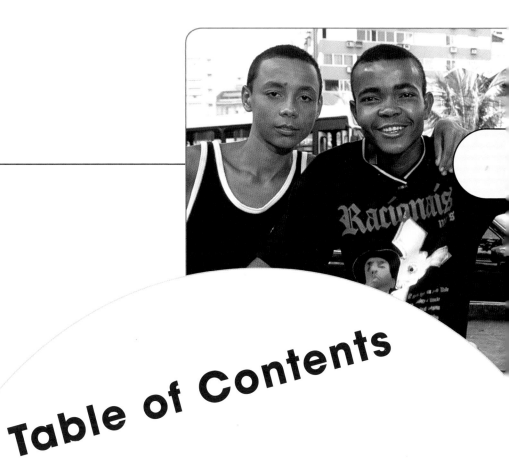

Table of Contents

Colorado

U.S.A.

Rio Grande

Mississippi

MEXICO

Gulf of Mexico

THE BAHAMAS

CUBA

BELIZE

GUATEMALA

JAMAICA

HONDURAS

HAITI

EL SALVADOR

DOM. REP.

NICARAGUA

Caribbean Sea

COSTA RICA

PANAMA

Orinoco

COLOMBIA

VENEZUELA

GUYANA

SURINAME

FRENCH GUIANA

ECUADOR

Amazon

Madeira

PERU

Brasilia

BRAZIL

BOLIVIA

PARAGUAY

CHILE

Paraná

ARGENTINA

URUGUAY

IRELAND
U.K.
BELGIUM LUX.
SWITZERLAND
FRANCE
ANDORRA
PORTUGAL
SPAIN
MOROCCO
Canary Islands
WESTERN SAHARA
MAURITANIA
SENEGAL
GAMBIA
GUINEA BISSAU GUINEA
SIERRA LEONE
LIBERIA

HUNGARY
AUSTRIA
BELGIUM LUX.
BULGARIA
TURKEY
SYRIA IRAQ
GREECE
ITALY
LEBANON
ISRAEL
SAUDI ARABIA

Mediterranean Sea

TUNISIA
LIBYA
EGYPT
Red Sea
Nile
ALGERIA
SUDAN
CHAD
MALI
NIGER
L. Chad
C.A.R.
Niger
BURKINA
NIGERIA
BENIN
TOGO
CAMEROON
GHANA
CONGO
IVORY COAST
EQUATORIAL GUINEA
CONGO
SAO TOME & PRINCIPE
GABON
Congo
ANGOLA

ATLANTIC
OCEAN

7

TEENS ARE A VITAL SEGMENT OF BRAZIL'S POPULATION, ONE THAT USES MUCH OF THE COUNTRY'S RESOURCES AND ALSO ONE WHOSE NEEDS THE GOVERNMENT CANNOT AFFORD TO IGNORE. Brazil ranks as the sixth most populated country in the world, with approximately 188 million residents. Teenagers account for more than 10 percent of that number—about 21 million are between the ages of 12 and 18.

Brazilian teens may be living in low-cost housing or in large, gated houses, but regardless of the type of home, the vast majority of Brazilians live in urban areas. About 22 percent live below the poverty line, while about 10 percent earn high incomes. Even though they are all Brazilians, the economic circumstances and lifestyles of teens there vary widely.

Lower secondary-school enrollment rates vary by region. In some rural areas it is less than 50 percent, while urban areas remain at 100 percent.

CHAPTER ONE

Attending School in Shifts

BY LAW, BRAZILIAN CHILDREN ARE REQUIRED TO ATTEND SCHOOL FROM AGES 7 TO 14 AND CANNOT WORK UNTIL THEY ARE 16. However, these laws are not always enforced. A majority of children in low-income Brazilian families, along with some middle-income families, work part time while attending school to help support their families. It is not unusual for these young people to begin working at age 10. In fact, more than 14 percent of children ages 10 to 14 are already in the labor force. There are also many children who work selling things on the streets, and their numbers are difficult to track.

Some of Brazil's working grade-school children and teens even drop out of school and work full time to help their families survive. New programs and a more flexible school schedule have encouraged more students to continue their education. In 2005, nearly 20 percent of students did not reach grade four of *primeiro grau*, or "primary school."

primeiro grau
pree-MAY-roo
graw

11

The Gol de Letra Foundation in São Paulo supports and promotes education for low-income children.

There are three main reasons for this relatively low rate of school attendance. First, many of Brazil's lower-income families desperately need the money that a teenager can earn working full time. Second, parents who did not attend much school themselves may not encourage their own children to stay in school. This practice tends to continue the cycle of illiteracy in a minority of the population. In 2004, for example, an estimated 12 percent of Brazilian adults, about 23 million, could not read or write. Third, a large number of Brazilian children are orphans and runaways who live in the streets and do not enroll themselves in school.

Homeless children known as *aban-donados* (meaning "abandoned ones") live on the streets of many of Brazil's cities. Some abandonados are forced to live on the streets when their parents die or abandon them. Others live and work on the streets to help support their families. To get

abandonados
ah-ban-doh-NAH-dohs

money, food, and other necessities, many abandonados sell inexpensive products on street corners. Some perform menial jobs such as shining shoes and carrying groceries, and still others survive by begging or stealing.

The considerably larger numbers of Brazilian young people who are not homeless and do attend high school, or segunda grau, usually choose from two general programs of study, depending on their plans for the future. Most students planning to go to college select the *colegial* program, which includes three years of courses designed to prepare them for attending a university. Other students choose a

segunda grau
se-GOON-dah graw
colegial
coh-le-GEE-al

The United Nations Children's Fund (UNICEF) has estimated that Brazil has 4.3 million orphans age 17 and under, most of whom live on the streets.

Teen Scenes

A 14-year-old girl lives in the Rocinha favela in Rio de Janeiro. Her house is modest, constructed of concrete, and consists of two rooms—a living room/kitchen area and a bedroom, which she shares with her mother.

She attends a school within her favela, and the courses include sewing and computer education.

She is active in her favela's samba school and spends much of her free time helping the school prepare for Carnival, by assisting in the building of the school's float and the sewing of the school's costumes.

Although she is busy with the samba school activities, she also helps her mother by selling candy from a stand on the street. Because she and her mother depend on the income this business generates, she must dedicate much of her time to making and selling the candy.

When she is not working at the samba school or the candy stand, she enjoys futebol, which she plays on the streets with her friends.

Another 14-year-old girl lives in Rio de Janeiro, but she is part of an upper-income family. Her parents have well-paying jobs, and her family lives in a large house that is surrounded by a fence with a locked gate.

A driver takes her to the private school she attends each day, dropping her off at the front door. Her courses include English and mathematics. She enjoys mathematics and hopes to one day be an engineer.

After school, a driver picks her up and takes her back home. Sometimes a few of her friends join her, and they all spend time hanging out at her house, chatting, surfing the Internet, or playing futebol in the yard.

Whether they are from low-income or high-income families, teens in Brazil enjoy time with friends, engaging in conversation and particpating in activities such as futebol.

Primary-School Enrollment Rates

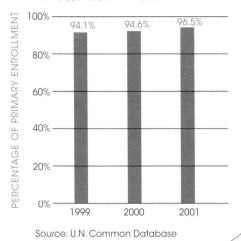

PERCENTAGE OF PRIMARY ENROLLMENT

- 94.1% (1999)
- 94.6% (2000)
- 96.5% (2001)

Source: U.N. Common Database

técnico
TAKE-nee-coh

técnico, or technical, school program. This three-year program prepares students to work in practical trades such as welding, tailoring clothes, or office work, including data processing. When they

graduate, they are ready to enter the work force.

Public Schools

Whether they are in high school or elementary school, most public school students in Brazil attend classes in two or three shifts. Each shift begins and ends at a different time of the day. Shifts were created because of over-crowded schools that cannot accommodate all of the enrolled students at the same time. This creative scheduling is one of the ways the government helps keep children in school.

Those young people scheduled for the morning shift typically begin classes at 7 A.M. and leave school at about 1 P.M. At that time, the second shift is about to begin. Students attending the afternoon shift leave school at 5 or 6 P.M. In those districts that have a night shift, the students begin classes at 7 P.M. and go home at 11 P.M. One advantage of

Students in Rio de Janeiro watch a state-produced television program during class time.

Despite Brazil's education-related problems, the country's literacy rate in 2004 was about 88 percent.

having three separate sessions of school is that students who need or want to work can choose a shift that does not interfere with their job hours. Despite having three shifts of classes, however, many Brazilian public school classrooms are still crowded.

It can be challenging to be a teacher in Brazil. A large proportion of Brazilian public school teachers are young and have very little education or training themselves. But this is starting to change.

In addition, most Brazilian public school teachers are not paid very well. A teacher's average pay in 2004 was between 214 and 428 reais (U.S.$100 and $200) per month, or about 2,570 to 5,142 reais (U.S.$1,202 to $2,404) per year, compared with the country's minimum wage of 350 reais (U.S.$164) per month. Under these conditions, it is not uncommon for teachers in various local areas to strike, refusing to work in order to get more money. That leaves students without teachers, sometimes for weeks at a time.

In spite of such problems, public schools in Brazil do manage to teach most of the enrolled students at least the basics of reading and writing. The vast majority of this basic learning takes place in the classroom. Homework is rarely assigned in public schools, partly because there are not enough textbooks and other school materials to supply all of the students. Also, teachers realize that many students have jobs outside of school and would not be able to complete homework on a regular basis.

Government Aid for Schools

The Brazilian government and private charities have been working to provide aid and creative incentives to make it easier for public school children, especially low-income ones, to attend school regularly. Among these incentives are free lunches, and, at some schools, free breakfasts. In Rio de Janeiro, food baskets are available for students to take home to their families.

Still another incentive is provided by a government program called Bolsa Escola. Needy families receive about 15 reais (U.S.$7) each month to replace the money their child could be earning by working full time. Families can get the money only if the students are in school full time and do not miss more than two days per month.

Teens eat lunch at the Esporto Club Ciudadano, a social project for low-income children.

Private Schools

Opportunities for learning are better in Brazil's private schools than in its public schools. The private schools have more money to spend on buildings, teachers, books, and other aspects of education. About 11 percent of the country's children, including a majority of those from upper-class families, along with some from middle-income families, go

in the public schools—approximately 2,137 reais (U.S.$984) per month. As a result, Brazil's better-educated and more experienced teachers tend to gravitate toward the private schools, where they can earn a better living.

The courses in private schools may include math, science, history, geography, and physical education. Brazil's private schools, like the country's public schools, also teach the native language, Portuguese. But students in the private schools are more likely to be offered instruction in other languages as well, especially English and Spanish. In fact, the vast majority of Brazilian private school students begin learning English from the time they start school at the age of 7.

Partly because there are enough textbooks for all the students and also because few of these students hold down jobs, teachers at private schools assign homework on most nights. In addition, many of the students who require extra help receive private tutoring outside of school, both in elementary and high school. The combination of more experienced teachers, regular homework assignments, and outside tutoring when needed often results in more learning than is possible in the average public school. In fact, students who attend Brazil's private schools are far more likely to go to college than their counterparts in the public schools.

Because they are usually better educated, private school students are also more likely to get higher-paying

to private schools. The average private school classroom has 20 to 30 students, considerably fewer than in most public schools. The private schools also pay their teachers a lot more than they could earn

jobs after they leave school, even if they do not go on to college.

Higher Education

Brazil's colleges recently experienced unprecedented growth in their student populations. About 25 percent of students attend public colleges, those funded by the government. One major benefit of attending the public colleges is that tuition is free for any and all Brazilians who pass the Vestibular exam, or college entrance exam. In contrast, private universities charge high tuitions, so they tend to attract mainly students who haven't scored well on the exam and who are from the country's wealthiest 10 percent of families. The public colleges have a somewhat more prestigious reputation than the private ones. This is partly because the public colleges usually offer more programs for advanced students—those seeking master's and doctoral degrees.

Students attend an internal medicine class at Rio de Janeiro State University.

Getting into College

Each December and January, those Brazilian students who have an interest in attending a university take a comprehensive college entrance exam called the Vestibular exam. Anyone who passes the test is guaranteed entrance into college. The exam is usually different for each area of study, so students must choose a major before taking the exam.

Some Brazilian teens attend a *cursinho pré-vestibular*, or cram school, before taking the Vestibular. These schools are expensive, so mainly students from higher-income families attend them. Cram schools help students learn the best ways to take the test and give practice tests to get them used to the kinds of questions that appear on the real test. Not surprisingly, when it comes time to take the Vestibular, those students who are able to attend cram schools score better than students who cannot. Because of this, there has been some controversy regarding the fairness of the exam.

cursinho pré-vestibular
cur-SEEN-nyo
pray-vay-STEE-bou-lar

21

The Brazilian government estimates that 84 percent of the country's population lives in urban areas.

2 Contrasting Lifestyles

BRAZIL IS A HIGHLY URBANIZED SOCIETY— MOST OF ITS INHABIT- ANTS DWELL IN CITIES. The living quarters occupied by the country's urban residents vary widely in quality.

Most members of higher-income families live in tall, attractive, well-main- tained apartment buildings. They often stand out in the skylines of major cities like Rio de Janeiro, São Paulo, and Salvador. In addition, some upper-income families dwell in spacious town- houses surrounded by walls that provide both privacy and security. It is common to see security guards stand- ing at the doors of the apartment buildings and the front gates of the town- houses. Inside these upscale homes, each family member

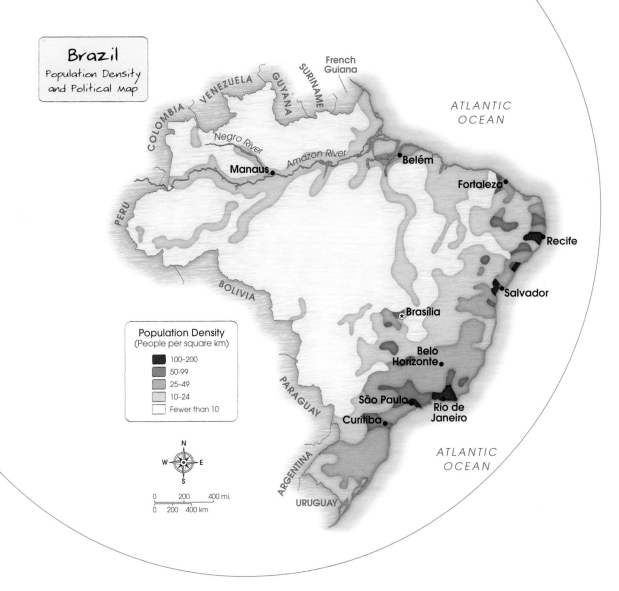

French
Guiana

*ATLANTIC
OCEAN*

VENEZUELA

SURINAME

GUYANA

COLOMBIA

Negro River

Amazon River

•Belém

Manaus•

Fortaleza•

PERU

•Recife

BOLIVIA

•Salvador

⊛Brasília

Population Density
(People per square km)

	100–200
	50–99
	25–49
	10–24
	Fewer than 10

Belo
Horizonte•

PARAGUAY

São Paulo•

•Rio de
Janeiro

Curitiba•

*ATLANTIC
OCEAN*

N
W • E
S

ARGENTINA

0   200   400 mi.
0   200   400 km

URUGUAY

generally has his or her own bedroom, and in the more expensive housing units, each family member often has a private bathroom as well. It is also common for each higher-income family to own several televisions and computers, along with all the latest modern conveniences.

Members of middle-income families in Brazilian cities also live in apartment buildings and houses. However, their homes usually feature fewer and smaller rooms and fewer amenities than those in higher-income neighborhoods. It is more common, for instance, for a middle-income home to have a single

An apartment complex in Minas Gerias is home to many middle-income families.

bathroom and possibly an additional half bath rather than several full baths. More than half of Brazil's middle-income urbanites can afford to hire a cook or a maid on either a part-time or full-time basis, because wages for those positions are not very high.

Some members of middle-income families, along with some in upper-income families, own their own cars.

However, even among these better-off families, car owners are in the minority—only about 12 percent of Brazilians buy their own automobiles. One reason for this relatively low percentage is that, with so many people living in the urban areas, a majority of them feel it is easier and cheaper to take buses, taxis, and other forms of public transportation common in the cities.

Life in the Favelas

In stark contrast to the situation in Brazil's upper- and middle-class urban neighborhoods—and sometimes only a few blocks away—are favelas stretching through large parts of the cities. A favela is a tenement block or urban quarter made up of slums or low-cost housing. More than 600 favelas exist in the city of Rio de Janeiro alone, each one home to hundreds of families. Favelas in Rio are getting larger each year. Between 1991 and 2000, for example, they grew by a rate of 4.5 percent per year.

The individual homes within an average favela are usually constructed by those who live in them, but sometimes the owners are aided by neighbors and friends. Wood and bamboo are the most common materials used, although pieces of recycled sheet metal, sheet-rock, plastic, and other materials are also employed. Roofs are typically made of sheets of corrugated metal, and floors are

The exact number of urban residents who live in favelas is unknown, but the government's and aid organizations' estimates vary from as low as 20 percent to as high as 40 percent.

Young residents of the Vila dos Papeleiros favela in Porto Alegre wash their hair at a public water tap.

either dirt or dirt covered with a layer of flagstones or throw rugs, or both.

Most houses in the favelas have only a few rooms—a small kitchen, a living room, and one or two bedrooms. With very few exceptions, neither the adults nor the children have their own rooms. When they can afford it, or when resources become available, many favela families manage to improve their homes. Thus, some of the older favelas may have homes that are a bit larger, more comfortable, and composed of more durable materials, such as brick or stone. These homes might also have a rudimentary system of pipes with running water, whereas most of the houses in the favelas lack this luxury. On the other hand, a majority of dwellings in these areas do have electricity, although typically it comes from illegal taps into city power lines. Very few residents of the favelas own cars. So the majority of young people living

Police officers patrol the Rocinha favela in Rio de Janeiro.

in these areas either walk or take city buses to work and school.

The favelas in Brazil's cities are more prone to crime and can be less safe than upper- and middle-income areas. As is true in large cities around the world, one cause of crime is the presence of drug dealers and gangs that operate and often thrive in the low-income neighborhoods of Brazilian cities. Out of fear of these criminal activities, it is common for nearly everyone in the favelas, from students to police officers, to carry guns and knives. So the sheer number of weapons on the streets makes violent incidents more likely.

In the majority of cases, police officers cannot enter a favela if they are called to resolve a dispute or solve a crime unless they have dozens of agents to back them up. Government presence in the favelas is almost non-existent, so in the majority of the cases, the *favelados* (people from the favelas)

CONTRASTING LIFESTYLES

favelados
fah-ve-LAH-dos

have created their own codes of conduct and means for justice to be administered. However, these informal ways of dealing with criminal conduct are ineffective and sometimes unjust.

In addition, some of the violence that occurs in the favelas, as well as in other parts of the cities, is directed against the large numbers of homeless teens and children. Many of these young people survive by stealing or committing other petty crimes. In an effort to reduce this problem, both ordinary citizens and police officers sometimes shoot young homeless people on sight. In 2003, more than 1,000 youths died this way in Rio de Janeiro alone. Because the police, and often city-dwellers in general, see such killings as ultimately beneficial to society, few of these incidents are fully investigated, and the killers are rarely prosecuted.

Because of the violence on the streets, the average life expectancy of a boy living in the Vale das Pedrinhas favela in Salvador, is just 25 years.

Rural Life in Brazil

As in the cities, there is a distinct division of economic classes and lifestyles in the rural areas of Brazil. In the countryside, wealthy citizens live on large estates, and members of middle-income families occupy small- to medium-size homes. The upper- and middle-income homes feature modern conveniences such as telephones, refrigerators, and computers. Hiring servants is common, especially among the wealthy, who can also afford to buy cars or trucks to get around.

In contrast, low-income families live in small homes with little or no running water or modern conveniences and, more often than not, must resort to bicycles, horses, or mules to get around. In the northern part of the country, where there are many rivers, boats are a common form of transportation for both upper- and lower-income families.

Regardless of how people in Brazil's rural areas live and get around, many do not stay long in these less-populated areas. In fact, in the last few decades, there has been a great deal of population movement in Brazil, particularly from the countryside into the cities. Between 2000 and 2005, Brazilian cities grew in population by a rate of about 1.8 percent per year.

Brazil
Topographical
Map

Water—Northern Brazil's Lifeline

Large sections of northern Brazil consist of rain forests that cannot be easily crossed by car or train. People who live in these areas typically get around by riding in boats on the Amazon River and its tributaries. Some of the more remote villages in the region are dependent on these boats for essential supplies of foodstuffs such as rice and beans. And major changes in weather patterns, especially rainfall amounts, can have serious consequences for the local residents.

For example, far less than the normal amount of rain fell during the winter of 2004–2005, which caused some of the local lakes and Amazon tributaries to dry up. Large supply boats were stranded in the middle of the rivers. Millions of fish and other animals died, ruining the drinking water for thousands of people. Even worse, more than 10,000 people were stranded, without access to any outside supplies, and the Brazilian armed forces had to fly supplies to the more remote villages. Helicopters dropped food, water, medical supplies, and chemicals to purify polluted supplies of drinking water.

In addition, the drought caused farmers to lose most of their crops. When the crops failed, the farmers could not pay their workers, and the poorest of these workers were forced to move to the cities in search of work.

At 4,049 miles (6,478 kilometers), the Amazon River is the second longest in the world. Only the Nile is longer. But the Amazon is the largest river in terms of volume.

The main reason for this migration is economic. Many rural folk feel they have few lucrative job opportunities, and so they seek better-paying jobs in the cities.

Among those in this group are an undetermined number of young people in their late teens who feel they are ready to strike out on their own. Some of them do find work in the cities and send part of their earnings back to their families in the countryside. Those who are unable to find work in the cities either return to their rural homes or remain and join the growing ranks of the urban homeless.

Staying Connected

Whether they live in the cities or the countryside, Brazilians of all walks of life stay connected to family, friends, employers, and others via phones. In 2004, Brazil had 42.3 million main telephone lines and 65.6 million cell phones in use. Bruno Noronha, a resident of São Paulo, said, "Here any child over the age of 10 has a cell phone. In a city like São Paulo, you want to know where your child is at all times and you want to be accessible at all times as well, so almost everyone has a cell phone."

Another way that a rapidly growing number of Brazilians stay connected is through the Internet. In 2005, Brazil had nearly 26 million Internet users. Bruno Noronha commented, "Teens use the Internet mainly to send e-mails, [and] use instant-messaging services, most commonly MSN. Nowadays instead of asking for someone's number, I have seen teens ask for their MSN address, and the national craze is to use the Web sites on where you have message boards and can contact your friends."

Most teenagers in upper-income homes have their own computers and enjoy Internet service. Teens in lower-income families have access to computers and the Internet in schools and public libraries. The lack of computer and Internet access for lower-income families is changing swiftly, however, thanks to the Brazilian government. It has ambitious plans to open roughly

Teens in São Paulo chat on their cell phones.

Teens use computers to do schoolwork, send e-mail messages, play video games, and shop.

6,000 community computer centers all across the country in 2007, with still more to come in the years that follow. Each center will offer word processing and Internet services free to children and teens. In addition, the government plans to distribute 1 million low-cost laptop computers per year to underprivileged school children beginning in 2007.

Meals

Another aspect of life in Brazil that connects urban and rural dwellers is the wide range of popular Brazilian foods. The majority of people in Brazil consume the same kinds of foods and have similar eating habits. For example, most Brazilians, including teens, eat a small breakfast, consisting of coffee and bread; this meal tends to be brief,

Spicing It Up with Feijoada

feijoada
fay-ju-AH-dah

couve
coh-u-VEE

farinha de mandioca
fah-REE-nya dee man-DEE-yoh-cah

farofa
fah-ROW-fah

Brazil's national dish—*feijoada*—consists of a spicy mix of black beans, pork, and sausage and is often eaten with *couve* (kale), slices of orange, and *farinha de mandioca* (a manioc flour). The dish has a long and rich history, beginning with the African slaves who worked on the country's farms and plantations when it was a European colony. The slaves ate a great deal of black beans, and when their masters occasionally gave them leftover pork, the slaves mixed the meat with the black beans. This tasty combination was soon adopted by other people living in Brazil, and some of them added sausage to the recipe. Others added *farofa*, or toasted manioc flour. Today individual recipes vary from region to region in the country, but virtually everyone eats some form of feijoada.

as family members hurry off to school or jobs. In contrast, lunch and dinner are often larger, more leisurely meals at which, when possible, all the members of the family gather around the table to eat and talk about the day's experiences.

The food consumed at lunch and dinner in Brazil has been heavily influenced by Portuguese culture, since people from Portugal were the first Europeans to settle the country. The cuisine has also been shaped by the cultures of African slaves, whom the Portuguese brought to Brazil. Among the main foods in that cuisine are grilled beef, pork, chicken, or fish, served with rice, beans, and a salad of lettuce and tomato. Brazilians also often eat stews made from fish and chicken.

Because the climate in most of Brazil is tropical, fresh fruits and vegetables are always available. Among the more popular fruits are bananas, papayas, pineapples, mangoes, apples, acerolas (fruit that resembles cherries), and *fruta-do-conde* (often called a sugar apple). Favorite vegetables include corn, yams, peppers, and manioc, a kind of cassava root. Because cassava root is often fried, it has sometimes been called the Brazilian version of french fries.

fruta-do-conde
FROO-tah du
COHN-dee

Fruta-do-conde is a popular fruit, and it's said that its flesh tastes like custard.

Tropical Rain Forest

The Amazon rain forest covers 40 percent of South America and spans eight countries—Brazil, Bolivia, Peru, Ecuador, Colombia, Venezuela, Guyana, and Suriname. The rain forest gets its name from the Amazon River and has the highest density of fish and birds in the world. It contains one third of Earth's animal life, including the harpy eagle, three-toed sloth, and anaconda.

The rain forest consists of four layers. The first layer is the emergent layer, where trees can reach heights of up to 200 feet (61 meters.) The second layer is the canopy, which is the main layer. The third layer is the understory, which houses the largest amount of insects. The fourth layer is the forest floor, where decomposing vegetation and organisms are broken down into nutrients for the soil.

Experts report that the Amazon rain forest is disappearing at a rate of 20,800 square miles (54,080 sq km) a year. More than 20 percent of the rain forest has already been destroyed. In addition, more than 90 indigenous tribes have been wiped out in Brazil alone since the coming of European colonists in the 1500s.

All of these kinds of meats, fruits, and vegetables are available at Brazilian grocery stores, although many people in the countryside get them from their own farms. Prepackaged foods familiar in other countries, such as frozen foods, pasta sauces, and ice cream, are also sold in grocery stores. Increasing numbers of Brazilians are turning to pre-packaged foods for some of their meals because they lead busy lives and such foods offer quicker, easier preparation.

Eating Out

Even faster and easier, of course, is eating out, especially at fast-food

Fast-food vendors sell food from carts.

Brazilian Coffee

Brazil is the world's largest coffee producer, supplying approximately one-third of the world's coffee. This booming industry started in 1727, when the Brazilian emperor announced that he was sending Francisco de Mello Palheta to French Guiana to settle a border dispute between the two countries. The real reason behind de Mello Palheta's visit, however, was to retrieve coffee seedlings from French Guiana. Although he was unable to obtain a coffee plant, he was able to charm the governor's wife. After settling the boundary dispute, he prepared to head home, receiving a bouquet of flowers from the governor's wife. De Mello Palheta discovered coffee seedlings hidden inside the bouquet, and he returned to Brazil with his prize.

Today Brazil is known for its mass production of coffee. In 2004, more than 16 million 132-pound (59-kilogram) bags were exported from Brazil. On average, each bag sold for 160 reais (U.S.$75), meaning the revenue for this profitable business topped more than 2 billion reais (U.S.$1 billion) in an eight-month span.

A worker in southeastern Brazil picks coffee beans by hand.

restaurants, which are particularly popular with teens and children. Such establishments have become widespread in Brazil in the last two decades, especially a number of foreign-based chains, including McDonald's, Dunkin' Donuts, and Domino's Pizza. Aside from the traditional beans and rice, pizza has become the most popular food in Brazil. In 2006, Starbucks became the newest foreign fast-food chain to reach Brazil. Among the more popular native Brazilian chains are Bob's, Habib's, and China in Box.

For their customers' convenience, many of these chains serve their food from kiosks—small, open-air structures—saving patrons from having to walk inside a building. Even McDonald's and Bob's have started serving their hamburgers from kiosks.

Street vendors are another ready source of fast food in Brazil, particularly in the cities. Selling everything from coffee and cake to full meals, the street vendors wheel their offerings around in carts or set up temporary stalls on sidewalks or street corners. Many of the stalls feature gas-powered grills on which the vendors prepare various meats and vegetables, as well as shish kebabs, for passersby. A few of the more successful vendors even set up portable tables and chairs so that their customers can sit comfortably while they eat.

In a similar vein, buffet-style restaurants are also very popular in Brazil. The buffets are housed in

Customers frequent the McDonald's restaurant in Salvador de Bahia.

Fast-food vendors put tables and chairs out for customers on a walkway in Rio de Janeiro

permanent shops that the customers enter from the street. Rather than charging one price per person for the buffets, these restaurants charge by the weight of the food. Brazil uses the metric system, so the weights are measured in kilograms. For that reason, many Brazilians use the nickname "kilos" to describe buffet restaurants.

A Land of Many Treats

Both the street vendors and buffets serve a wide variety of pastries. More than a breakfast food in Brazil, pastries are often eaten as desserts, treats, and in some cases even as entire meals. Brazilians fill their dessert pastries with chocolate, caramel, and other sweets, while they stuff cheese, chicken, and

A teen living in the Amazon rain forest prepares a meal in an open kitchen.

pork into large pastries that become main dinner courses. Another popular pastry, the *pastel frito*, is a small turnover—a pocket of dough stuffed with tasty fillings such as beef or shrimp—that is eaten as a snack or appetizer.

Pastries are not the only popular foods consumed as snacks, appetizers, and desserts

pastel frito
paz-TEWL
FREE-too

Pão de queijo are made with tapioca starch or flour, parmesan cheese, milk, eggs, and sometimes potatoes.

in Brazil. Another favorite fare, both at home and when eating out, is *pão de queijo*, cheese bread rolls. Other popular snacks include bacon-flavored popcorn; *curau*, a sweet puddinglike dessert made with corn; and ice cream. Among the more popular flavors of curau are those featuring tropical fruits—such as guava, passion fruit, and mango—as well as coconut, Brazil nut, peanut, avocado, and corn.

pão de queijo
paw-dee KAY-ju

curau
CU-rauh

43

Members of Brazilian families usually remain close throughout their lives.

3

Benefits of Family Ties

TIES OF FAMILY AND FRIENDSHIP IN BRAZIL ARE STRONG AND EXTEND THROUGH ALL SOCIAL CLASSES AND ECONOMIC GROUPS— from luxury high-rise apartments in the cities, to the poorest favelas, to towns and villages stretching across the countryside. On one level, such ties form satisfying bonds based on love, respect, and mutual admiration. On another level, relationships among family and friends form a social network that helps keep Brazilian society functioning smoothly.

A large proportion of this network consists of people in various walks of life doing favors for their friends and family whenever possible. For example, city-dwellers often provide

A group of friends hang out in Rio de Janeiro.

lodging for the teenage sons and daughters of friends and relatives from the countryside so that these young people can work or attend school in the cities. Similarly, shopkeepers and farmers frequently offer jobs or financial deals to people they know, and restaurant owners and workers save tables for their friends.

Family Ties

The roots of this countrywide network of interrelationships and cooperation can be found in the home, the focal point of Brazil's central social and economic unit: the family. In some Brazilian families—spanning the wealthy, middle-, and lower-income classes—it is common for aunts, uncles, and cousins, as well as grandparents, to live in one house.

Grandparents and older parents in such families are generally respected for their age, experience, and knowledge, and children and teens in the family are expected to obey them. Brazilian grandparents often contribute to the family's income. If they worked for many years and then retired with social security benefits, they commonly share those benefits with other family members. The average age of retirement in Brazil is 59.8 for men and 54 for women (compared with global averages of 61 for men and 57 for women). In other cases, parents and grandparents reject the notion of retiring and continue working. The exact number of grandparents and elderly people in Brazil who do not retire and continue bringing money into the family unit is unknown.

Teens and other family members benefit from the help, experience, and earning power of others besides grandparents. When a Brazilian teen wants

Brazil has one of the fastest growing elderly populations in the world.

The connections that a network of friends in Brazil can offer are important for many aspects of a teenager's life.

to learn to drive, or to acquire a job, or to find a place to live, for instance, he or she typically turns to older relatives, such as fathers, older brothers, or uncles, for help. Similarly, it is not unusual for wealthy and middle-class Brazilians to assist their low-income relatives by helping them find jobs or lending them money. In fact, it is quite common for large groups of relatives to work together in the same company or on the same farm.

The Importance of Friendships

Teens and other young people in Brazil also turn to trusted neighbors and friends for companionship and emotional support, as well as for social and economic connections and help. Young friends engage in numerous

Staying Out Late With Friends

In Brazil, curfews are rare for teenagers, partly because many teens both work and attend school, sometimes on schedules that require being away from home during the evening. Also, in many cases, evening is the only time that friends can get together. One exception to the relaxed attitude about curfews is the way some parents treat their daughters. Some families impose curfews for teenage girls, while allowing the boys to stay out as late as they please.

activities together, including attending school, going to the movies and concerts, playing sports, hanging out at the beach, and dating. And as friends do in all places and times, they offer one another comfort and encouragement in everyday life and share personal problems and secrets. Some of these relationships remain strong for life.

Tens of thousands of participants and spectators flock to the Sambódromo in Rio de Janeiro during Carnival.

4 Carnival & Celebrations

BRAZILIANS OF ALL AGES ARE ALWAYS HAPPY TO HAVE SOMETHING TO CELEBRATE. Among the many social and family occasions regularly celebrated in Brazil are birthdays, graduations, weddings, baptisms, and other religious observances. All of these celebrations involve parties, feasts, or other get-togethers at which family and friends enjoy food, music, and fun.

Many of these celebrations are religious in nature, most often tied to the Roman Catholic Church. After all, more than 70 percent of the people who live in Brazil are Roman Catholics, and many of the country's cities are named for Christian saints. Some familiar examples are São Sebastião and São Jorge. The residents of these cities celebrate their saint's name day, along with national holidays and festivities such as Christmas, Easter, and Carnival.

National Holidays in Brazil

Confraternização Universal, Año Novo (New Year's Day)—January 1

Carnival—Tuesday before Ash Wednesday, but festivities begin on the preceding Friday

Quarta-feira de Cinzas (Ash Wednesday)—the first day of Lent

Sexta-Feira da Paixão, Sexta Feira Santa (Good Friday)—Friday before Easter

Páscoa (Easter)—the Sunday after Good Friday

Tiradentes—April 21   Honors Brazilian hero who led unsuccessful revolt against Portuguese rule

Dia do Trabalho (Labor Day)—May 1

Corpus Christi—62 days after Good Friday

Dia da Independência (Independence Day)—September 7

Nossa Senhora de Aparecida (Our Lady of Aparecida)—October 12

Proclamação da República (Proclamation of the Republic Day)—November 15

Natal (Christmas)—December 25

Religion in Brazil

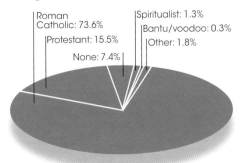

Roman Catholic: 73.6%
Protestant: 15.5%
None: 7.4%
Spiritualist: 1.3%
Bantu/voodoo: 0.3%
Other: 1.8%

Source: United States Central Intelligence Agency. *The World Factbook—Brazil.*

Carnival: Partying in the Streets

One of the biggest and most anticipated holidays in Brazil is Carnival. It is held during the five days before Ash Wednesday. For Brazilians and other Christians around the world, Lent is a time of sacrifice and sobriety before Easter, which is celebrated as the day Christ rose from the dead. It is one of the few periods in Brazil's calendar

A single samba school will spend an entire year preparing its float and costumes for Rio de Janeiro's Carnival.

in which partying is uncommon, until Carnival. The word Carnival originally meant "goodbye to meat," because in traditional Portuguese society no one ate meat during the 40 days preceding Easter. The term *carnival* is used throughout Brazil to denote not only the holiday but also each individual celebration of it. These individual carnivals occur in every region, city, and town in the country. Each is slightly different, with variations based on local customs, but all resemble, to one degree or another, the world-famous version held in Rio de Janeiro.

Each year in Rio, a man is elected to be Rei Momo, king of Carnival, charged with leading the festivities and riding or walking at the front of several parades. The largest parade in Rio winds through an area called the Sambódromo, a structure lined with permanent grandstands. Tens of thousands of people come from other parts of the country and from around the world to watch the festivities.

The main parade in Rio's Carnival always features performances by several

Samba Schools

Samba schools are not actually teaching institutions but rather local, neighborhood-based social clubs, usually in favelas. Samba schools provide valuable jobs for their neighborhoods, employing people year-round producing costumes and floats for Carnival, which takes place before Quarta-feira de Cinzas (Ash Wednesday). The best 14 schools are invited to compete at the Sambódromo, a 1-mile (1.6-km) long concrete parade ground built in the center of Rio de Janeiro specifically for Carnival. Schools that aren't invited perform in the streets. Rehearsals for Carnival begin in mid-September or early October. Each school must create an original dance honoring a historic person or event, with costumes, songs, and a parade float relevant to the chosen theme. Each school has between 60 and 85 minutes to perform during the parade.

During the two weeks leading up to Carnival, groups called *blocos* go around the neighborhood playing music and singing and dancing. Bystanders are invited to participate. Some blocos are so famous that they draw followers in the tens of thousands.

The Friday before Quarta-feira de Cinzas, many lavish balls take place. Once for the elite only, now all can participate if they're willing to pay the high prices. Finally, the parade of samba schools in the Sambódromo begins. The parade starts on Sunday at 9 P.M. and can go until 6 A.M. or 7 A.M. the next day. Schools bring thousands of members to perform in the parade, which draws 60,000 spectators and millions more watching on TV.

blocos
BLOH-coos

The largest and most prestigious samba schools can have as many as 7,000 members.

of the city's samba schools. These are social or cultural groups that meet on a regular basis to learn and ultimately to perform traditional Brazilian samba music. The members of each local samba school, which represents an individual neighborhood, vary in number. All those involved work diligently throughout each year preparing music, dance routines, and costumes that will be shown off in Rio's Carnival.

The quality of these performances is seen as crucial because the various samba schools compete at Carnival, and the winner receives prize money, along with considerable fame. During the big parade, each samba school passes through the Sambódromo, and a panel of judges rates each school's performance to choose the winner for that year. Each school also marches through and performs for its own neighborhood

For one night, on Carnival, the samba schools from the favelas are the focus of thousands of upper- and middle-income Brazilians.

during the many regional street parties that take place during Carnival.

In Rio's favelas, as well as in the favelas of other Brazilian cities, samba schools are a source of fun for people of all ages who lack the money to attend formal theaters and concerts. Children and teens learn how to dance and play instruments in the samba schools. They also help their parents and other older relatives and friends sew costumes and create floats and decorations for the parades. Indeed, both inside and outside the favelas, working on Carnival is a community activity that affords teens and others an enjoyable way to spend their leisure time.

Páscoa

After Carnival is over, Brazilians look forward to a number of more solemn observances that take place during the week before Páscoa, or Easter. During Semana Santa, or Holy Week, people across the country prepare a special food called *pacoca*. This tasty candy—made from crushed nuts, sugar, and other ingredients—is a traditional gift offered to friends and family who come to visit during the Easter holidays.

On Palm Sunday (the Sunday before Easter), the Catholic churches in Brazil and throughout the world hold services during which priests bless palm leaves. These leaves symbolize the palms that, according to the Bible, crowds of Jews waved as Jesus entered Jerusalem shortly before being crucified by the Romans. Following a similar Christian tradition, on

pacoca
pah-COH-cah

A teenager dresses as an angel for Semana Santa celebrations in southeastern Brazil.

57

Rio de Janeiro's citizens display one of the world's largest Christmas trees, which is nearly 271 feet (83 meters) tall.

Good Friday (the Friday before Easter), a somber funeral procession winds its way through many Brazilian villages and cities. The marchers carry a replica of Jesus' body and a statue of Mary. In addition, each year since 1950 the village of Nova Fazenda, located in west-central Brazil, presents a passion play in which volunteers act out Jesus' arrest, trial, and execution.

Natal

Because Brazil lies south of the equator, December through March are considered summer months, while June through September are winter months. So Natal, or Christmas, falls during the hottest part of the year. Children and younger teens receive gifts from Papai Noel, who supposedly lives in Greenland. When he visits Brazil, he

St. Francis Church in Salvador has an open stage for Christmas plays during the Natal season.

wears silk clothing to stay cool. Most families decorate their homes with fresh flowers, as well as Christmas trees.

Other highlights of Brazil's Natal season include colorful pageants and decorative displays. Pageants tell the story of Jesus' birth in Bethlehem and are presented in schools across the nation, as well as by various community organizations and private groups. Also widely popular are Presépios. These, manger scenes show the baby Jesus, his mother, and the animals, shepherds, and wise men who visited him, according to the traditional biblical Christmas story. Presépios of various sizes and degrees of detail can be seen both inside and outside of many Brazilian churches, stores, and homes.

On Christmas Eve, Roman Catholics attend the Missa do Galo, or "Mass of the rooster." It is so named because it ends well past midnight, when, according to tradition, roosters crow to welcome the coming of dawn. As a result, large numbers of Brazilians either get little or no sleep on Christmas Eve and Christmas morning. Some may sleep late on Christmas morning.

Many families celebrate Natal by spending the afternoon preparing for the evening Ceia de Natal, or Christmas dinner. Some Brazilians eat their holiday dinner shortly after attending the Christmas Eve Mass. Most revelers eat Brazil's traditional Christmas fare, consisting of turkey, sometimes accompanied by ham, served with colored rice and large platters piled with mixtures of fresh vegetables and fruits.

The minimum wage in Brazil is 350 reais (U.S.$164) per month.

5

Education Brings Better Jobs

LARGE NUMBERS OF BRAZILIANS WORK AT VARIOUS JOBS, EVEN IF PART TIME, FROM A YOUNG AGE. Exact figures for child labor in Brazil are unknown, but as of 2003, UNICEF estimated that 7 percent of children between the ages of 5 and 17 worked. These children and teens frequently manage to juggle both school and work.

In most cases, youngsters who work the longest hours are helping their parents in whatever line of work the parents are in. For example, in the countryside, it is common for children and teens to labor alongside their parents in coal and copper mines. Other young rural Brazilians tend and harvest crops of sugarcane, oranges, wheat, rice, corn, and soybeans on farms owned by their parents, relatives, or friends of

Division of Labor

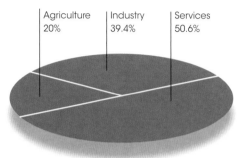

| Agriculture 20% | Industry 39.4% | Services 50.6% |

Source: United States Central Intelligence Agency. *The World Factbook—Brazil.*

the family. In the cities, young workers are often employed in the homes of the wealthy, cleaning houses, washing clothes, doing yard work, and washing cars. Still other urban teens work in shops, stocking shelves and sweeping.

A teen in Juruena makes deliveries on his bicycle.

EDUCATION BRINGS BETTER JOBS

A young woman in the Rocinha favela in Rio de Janeiro sells handmade soaps from a shop on the street.

Work for Brazilian Teens and Adults

Eventually, those teens who hold down part-time jobs graduate to full-time employment, either by dropping out of school or finding full-time work after high school graduation. In this way, they join the country's full-time adult labor force.

Overall, whether they are youngsters or adults, only about a third of Brazil's workers are in jobs that are viewed as legal by the government. Legal jobs are generally defined as those that offer an official employment contract that requires those who sign it to pay social security (deducted from each paycheck) and that guarantees the worker will receive social security benefits upon retiring. The rest of the workers in the country are either self-employed or work for someone else without a legal contract. No one tries to stop them from working, but it is understood that they

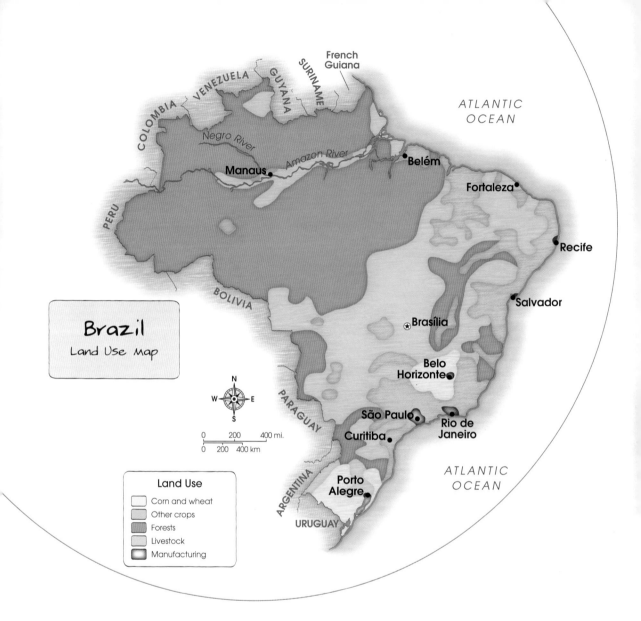

Brazil
Land Use Map

Land Use
- Corn and wheat
- Other crops
- Forests
- Livestock
- Manufacturing

must fend for themselves if they decide to retire.

More Education Means More Opportunities

Education is often the key to the best career opportunities. With occasional exceptions, those who are better educated have more opportunities for earning and advancement in the workplace. For example, young people who complete primary school usually get better-paying jobs than those who do not finish primary school. Their

A teenager walks on a Rio de Janeiro beach, selling watermelon.

ability to read makes them eligible for restaurant and office work. Those who cannot read or who have poor reading skills tend to do more menial labor, such as digging ditches, picking fruit in the fields, and tapping rubber trees on rubber plantations.

In contrast, young people who graduate from technical high schools generally find higher-paying jobs than those who only complete primary school. Technical school graduates are qualified to work in relatively high-paying trades. These include electricians, plumbers, data-entry clerks, and assembly-line managers in factories. Even more higher-paying positions in the workforce are open to Brazilians who go on to finish college—among them lawyers, accountants, doctors, scientists, and computer programmers.

Futebol is the nation's most popular sport.

6

CHAPTER SIX

A Passion for Play

NO MATTER HOW MANY HOURS PER WEEK BRAZILIANS DEVOTE TO WORK, SCHOOL, AND OTHER SERIOUS ACTIVITIES, MOST STILL MANAGE TO FIND TIME FOR A LITTLE FUN. By far the two top leisure pastimes in Brazil—for both teens and adults—are samba and *futebol* (soccer). Large numbers of urban youths of all ages, whether they come from higher- or lower-income families, spend a lot of their free time in local samba schools preparing for Carnival. Meanwhile, nearly all young people—both boys and girls, living in cities and rural areas—play futebol. Thousands of informal games are held daily on school grounds, in parks, on roadways, in the favelas, and even on beaches. In addition, children and teens, along with

futebol
fu-tee-BOW

67

Brazilian teens love to play futebol on the beach.

their parents and grandparents, watch professional futebol matches on TV and regularly discuss the latest scores and team standings.

A National Obsession

Professional futebol might be more accurately described as a national craze or obsession among the majority of Brazilians. The nation's ongoing futebol rivalry with neighboring Argentina has actually caused riots, and during the World Cup competition many Brazilian businesses close to allow employees to stay home to watch the matches on television. The Brazilian team colors are yellow and green—the colors of the national flag.

The country is known for producing excellent futebol players. One of

Brazil's most popular homegrown players, Ronaldinho, plays for FC Barcelona. He has twice (2004 and 2005) been named Fédération Internationale de Football Association (FIFA) World Player of the Year. Other successful and popular Brazilian futebol players include Rivaldo Vitor Borba Ferreira and Ronaldo Luíz Nazário de Lima.

But their fame pales before that of another Brazilian player who is widely acknowledged as the world's greatest and most legendary futebol athlete. Named for Thomas Edison, the American inventor of the lightbulb, Edson Arantes do Nascimento is better known by his nickname—Pelé. He is also sometimes called O Rei do Futebol, "the king of soccer." During his career,

Pelé celebrated after scoring three consecutive goals during a Cosmos home game at Giants Stadium.

Pelé

Pelé's story gives teens in Brazil's favelas hope. He grew up in poverty and managed to achieve fame and fortune through talent, hard work, and perseverance. Born in 1940 in Três Corações, a city in southeastern Brazil, Pelé came from a family so poor that he did not own a real soccer ball. Instead, he stuffed paper into a sock and used this makeshift ball for practice. When he was 11, a well-known futebol scout noticed his talent and began promoting him. By age 16, Pelé was the leading scorer in the Brazilian league. He retired from Brazilian futebol in 1974, but promptly came out of retirement to play for the New York Cosmos, earning a then unprecedented sum of $7 million a year. He retired permanently in 1977, having scored nearly 1,300 goals in his spectacular career.

Brazilian skateboarder Lincoln Ueda performs at international skateboarding events.

he won three World Cup medals and set several world records.

High-Flying Skateboarders

Among the other widely played sports and other leisure pastimes in Brazil are surfing, volleyball, skateboarding, and Capoeira, a kind of martial art. The latter two are by far the most popular sports

after futebol.

Skateboarding is more popular in Brazil than it is in most other countries. If Brazilian teens can afford a skateboard and display a high degree of skill at the sport, they can hope to attract the attention of world-renowned skateboarders like American Tony Hawk. He asked Brazilian skateboarder Lincoln Ueda to perform in his annual tour in 2003, 2004, and 2005. The young Brazilian thrilled crowds with his agility, speed, and ability to fly higher into the air than most of his competitors. "Lincoln is one of the most exciting skaters out there," Hawk said. "When you see the passion and dedication of these Brazilian guys, it's inevitable they would reach the top ranks."

Among the other "Brazilian guys" cited by Hawk are Sandro Dias and Bob Burnquist. Like Ueda, they moved to the United States to help promote their skateboarding careers, and all three make a point of supporting younger Brazilian skateboarders who want to make it big in the sport. Partly because of these favors extended to fellow countrymen, there is usually a Brazilian skateboarder in one of the top three spots in most international skateboarding competitions.

A Tricky Form of Self-defense

At least equal to skateboarding in popularity among young Brazilians, Capoeira originated with the African slaves who were forced to come to Brazil in the country's colonial days. The slaves wanted to practice a disciplined martial art in their few work-free hours on the plantations. But their masters, who worried that this would empower the slaves and cause uprisings, forbade them from doing so. In response, the slaves cleverly disguised their Capoeira moves as dance steps. And

Capoeira may look like a dance, but it is a form of self-defense.

Capoeira pants are called abadas.

for this reason the art, sport, or game of Capoeira became in a very real way a fascinating combination of formalized fighting and acrobatic dancing, featuring numerous graceful kicks, leaps, and spins.

Today in Brazil, teens and young adults often practice Capoeira in local athletic clubs and gyms, which stage annual meets and competitions with rival clubs. But the game is equally

abadas
ah-BA-dahs

popular on the streets, much as back-lot baseball and basketball are among young people in the United States.

Whether staged formally in clubs or informally on the streets, Capoeira is played inside a circle called a *roda*. The object is not to hurt one's opponent, but rather to match one's strategy, tactics, and agility to those of the opponent. The most basic movement is a side-to-side rocking motion called the *ginga*, consisting of a series of cautious, measured swinging motions. This movement prepares the player for his or her attack, which can variously include moves such as kicks and sweeps, ducks and rolls, cartwheels, handstands, head- or handspins, flips, jumps, and turns. There are an equal number of defensive moves to counter these attacks.

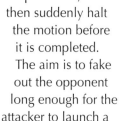

roda
HROW-dah

ginga
JEEN-gah

The most skilled Capoeira students frequently attempt to trick their opponents. The art of trickery in the game is referred to as *malandragem* and consists of various mock blows or attacks and fakes intended to throw an opponent off guard and cause him or her to make a mistake. For instance, one might initiate a motion, wait for the other player to respond to it, and then suddenly halt the motion before it is completed. The aim is to fake out the opponent long enough for the attacker to launch a new motion, this time one that follows through and wins the match.

malandragem
mah-lan-DRAH-gien

During the execution of all these attacks, defensive moves, and fakes, the Capoeira players are accompanied by catchy music, which first developed during the era in which the slaves transformed the sport into a dancelike

display. The music is typically played on several kinds of instruments. The rhythm is led by the *berimbaus*, which looks like an archer's bow. When the player strikes the string with a wooden stick, it produces a buzzing sound, a high sound, or a sound like that of a plucked guitar. The other instruments include tambourines, a

berimbaus
bay-reen-BAH-uz

Samba students at Samba School Viradouro rehearse for Carnival.

Popular Music

Axé Artist
Ivete Sangalo

Axé music (Ah-sh-eh), sometimes called "samba reggae," originated in Salvador, Bahia, Brazil. It began as a mix of Afro-Brazilian samba with electronic instruments, and quickly became a popular form of dance music.

Funk Artists
MC Serginho
MC Tati Quebra Barraco
MC Leozinho

Brazilian funk is very different from the kind of funk music found in most other places. Developed mostly in the favelas, it has lyrics that are explicit and is seen by many of the middle class as an aggressive and violent form of music.

Techno Artists
Alvinho L. Noise
Renato Cohen

Techno is a form of electronic dance music that is mainly instrumental. This makes it ideal for DJs who play long sets. In Brazil top DJs from around the world always attract large crowds at clubs and raves.

Ivete Sangalo performed at the annual Rock in Rio music festival.

Samba Artists
Wilson Moreira (samba)
Inimigos da HP (pagode)
Nora Ney (samba-canção)

Brazil's national music style, samba, was developed by black immigrants of Bahia. Today there are many offshoot varieties, including axé (samba reggae), pagode, which is characterized by playful or funny lyrics, and samba-canção, a slower, more romantic style.

rasp, a double-gong bell, and sometimes a drum.

A number of songs composed especially for Capoeira matches have become widely popular in Brazil. Teens and young adults who follow the sport particularly like the music, but it is also popular among people of all ages around the country. Some of these songs have even become familiar outside Brazil.

More Music and Dancing

Various types of music and dance are popular among Brazilian teens and young adults, as well as among the young at heart of all ages. Dance clubs are popular places for teens to groove. Bruno Noronha said, "Most teens from around the age of 16 start going to night clubs to dance and have a good time. Some of these clubs open their doors on Sundays for matinees that start at 6 and end at midnight."

Samba music and the dance moves that often accompany it are, of course, a major crowd-pleaser during Carnival and other celebrations. Also widely popular is the tango, a stately

Dancing is a popular pastime in Brazil.

ballroom dance that originated in neighboring Argentina. Another popular dance, the bossa nova, started in Brazil. Samba, tango, and bossa nova rhythms and songs are familiar to and beloved by Brazilians of all ages. They are frequently played on the radio and at dances and parties. These older, more traditional musical and dance forms are an integral part of the culture.

Even so, Brazilian teens are considerably more interested in contemporary rock 'n' roll and pop music. Some artists and bands popular among young people in Brazil are native-born. Among them are Os Mutantes, Ira!, Capital Inicial, and a number of heavy-metal and punk groups that got their start in clubs in Rio and other Brazilian cities. Equally and sometimes even more popular among Brazilian teens are American pop artists and bands, particularly Snoop Dogg, Wu-Tang Clan, OutKast, Insane Clown Posse, and P. Diddy.

Information and Entertainment

Another leisure activity that Brazilians of all ages enjoy is watching television.

Television sets can be found in most Brazilian homes and even along the streets.

At least 90 percent of Brazil's homes have at least one TV. People watch to learn what is happening in their country and the world and to be entertained by sporting events, comedies, and dramas. The high number of television sets can be attributed to the military government of the 1960s and 1970s. During that

A teen on the street watches the televisions on display in a shop.

Brazil's national futebol team is ranked number one by FIFA and has won the FIFA World Cup five times.

time, the government offered television sets to the public through many installment payments. The main programming on TV was offered by Rede Globo, a station that supported the military goals and ideals of the government.

Among the leading television programs today, major futebol matches, especially those in the World Cup contests, draw the most viewers. However,

young people regularly discuss the latest story lines and character dilemmas in school, on school buses, and at work. The telenovelas generally begin around 7 or 8 P.M., and each plays for an hour, six nights a week. Each story line, or "novel," lasts for about six months, after which a new story begins.

The more popular Brazilian soaps in recent years have been *Terra Nostra* (*Our Land*) in 2003, *A Escrava Isaura* (*Slave Isaura*) in 2004, and *Alma Gêmea* (*Twin Soul*) in 2005 and 2006. All three, along with others, gained followings in several other countries as well.

Movies are popular in Brazil, though less so than television, in part because television is free and movies can be costly for lower-income Brazilians. Still, movies are shown all over the country and are usually well-attended. Although some native Brazilian films achieved high popularity in recent years—notably *Central do Brasil* and *Cidade de Deus* (*City of God*)—in general Brazilian moviegoers tend to prefer foreign films, particularly American ones.

a close second in popularity are Brazil's TV soap operas, the *telenovelas*, or "television novels." Teens, mainly girls but also some boys, quite often watch these shows with their parents, and

81

Looking Ahead

BRAZILIAN TEENS HAVE RICH CULTURAL traditions that their own children will be privileged to inherit. Religious ceremonies, holidays, and feasts; family get-togethers; the samba schools and the yearly Carnival; the Capoeira tournaments; and the ongoing exploits of Brazil's leading futebol teams are only some of the traditions enjoyed by Brazilians of all ages and walks of life. Like their parents and grandparents before them, the country's teens have a great deal of pride in their culture and its traditions.

Although there remains much poverty in Brazil, each year the country's standard of living rises a bit. Part of this positive trend is reflected in the fact that each year a slightly higher percentage of Brazilian children attend school than in previous years. Moreover, increasing numbers of students stay in school for at least several years. Experts predict that this will cause the country's current adult-literacy rate of about 88 percent to rise well into the 90 percent range in the next decade or two. Brazilian teens know that more education means more opportunities. Increasing numbers of teens are graduating from high school and are preparing to lead their country to a prosperous future.

At a Glance

At a Glance

Official name: Federative Republic of Brazil

Capital: Brasilia

People

Population: 188,078,227

Population by age group:
0–14 years: 25.8%
15–64 years: 68.1%
65 years and over: 6.1%

Life expectancy at birth: 71.97 years

Official language: Portuguese

Other languages: Several indigenous languages; small groups of immigrants speak their native languages

Religions:
Roman Catholic: 73.6%
Protestant: 15.4%
Spiritualist: 1.3%
Bantu/voodoo: 0.3%
Other: 1.8%
Unspecified: 0.2%
None: 7.4%

Legal ages:
Alcohol consumption: 18
Driver's license: 18
Military service: 18
Voting: 16

Government

Type of government: Federative Republic

Chief of state and head of government: President and vice president, elected by popular vote

Lawmaking body: Congresso Nacional or Bicameral National Congress, consisting of the Federal Senate and the Chamber of Deputies

Administrative divisions: 26 states and one federal district

Independence: Declared September 7, 1822; recognized August 29, 1825 (from Portugal)

National symbols: Stars on the flag represent the 26 states and one federal district

Geography

Climate: Tropical, temperate in the south

Total area: 3,404,786 square miles (8,852,444 square kilometers)

Major landforms: Amazon rain forest, the Patanal, coastal mountains, central plains

Major rivers: Amazon, Paraná, Iguaçu, Negro, São Francisco, Xingu, Madeira, Tapajós

Highest point: Pico da Neblina, 9,946 feet (3,034 meters)

Lowest point: Atlantic Ocean, sea level

Economy

Currency: Brazilian real (plural is reais)

Population below poverty line: 22%

Major natural resources: Bauxite, gold, iron ore, manganese, nickel, phosphates, platinum, tin, uranium, petroleum, hydropower, timber, coffee, soybeans, wheat, rice, corn, sugarcane, cocoa, citrus

Major agricultural products: Coffee, soybeans, wheat, rice, corn, sugarcane, cocoa, citrus, beef

Major exports: Transportation equipment, iron ore, soybeans, footwear, coffee, automobiles

Major imports: Machinery, electrical and transportation equipment, chemical products, oil

Historical Timeline

Women gain voting privileges in New Zealand, the first country to take such a step

Bronze Age well established in Europe

James Watt patents the steam engine, initiating the Industrial Revolution

Slavery is abolished; the monarchy is overthrown the following year and a federal republic controlled by coffee interests is established

| 5000 B.C. | 2000 B.C. | A.D. 1500 | 1600s | 1769 | 1822 | 1888 | 1893 |

Seminomadic indigenous people populate a wide area of present-day Brazil

British colonies are established in North America

Son of the Portuguese king declares independence for Brazil and crowns himself Peter I, Emperor of Brazil

Portuguese explorer Pedro Álvares Cabral arrives in Brazil; the Portuguese begin settlement

 Historical World Event

Revolt brings dictator Getúlio
Vargas to power; he is ousted
in a 1945 military coup but
elected president in 1951; he
commits suicide in 1954 after
military gives him options of
resigning or being overthrown

President Joao Goulart is
ousted by the military
in bloodless coup;
repression and rapid
economic growth follow

 The United Nations
is founded

 Two U.S.
astronauts land
on the moon

1929   1930   1943   1945   1950–1953   1956–1961   1964   1969

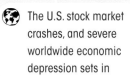 The U.S. stock market
crashes, and severe
worldwide economic
depression sets in

 The Korean War

Brazil experiences rapid
economic growth under
President Juscelino
Kubitschek; he moves
the capital from Rio de
Janeiro to Brasília
in 1960

Brazil joins the Allies in
World War II (1939–1945)

Historical Timeline

Tancredo Neves is elected the first civilian president in 21 years, but dies before taking office; Vice President Jose Sarney becomes president at a time of economic crisis, with inflation at 300 percent

Series of prison uprisings sparks deadly gang attacks and police backlash; President Lula is re-elected

🌐 Terrorist attacks on the two World Trade Center Towers in New York City and on the Pentagon in Washington, D.C., leave thousands dead

Brazil launches its first space rocket; a launch attempt the previous year caused an explosion that killed 21 people

1981   1985   1991   2000   2001   2002   2004   2006

🌐 Soviet Union collapses

Soccer fans jubilant as Brazil wins the World Cup for the fifth time; Luiz Inacio Lula da Silva, known as Lula, wins the presidential election and leads first left-wing government in more than 40 years

🌐 The first personal computer in the world is introduced

Celebrations of Brazil's 500th anniversary marred by protests by indigenous Indians who say that genocide, forced labor, and disease have slashed their population from 5 million before the Portuguese arrived to 350,000

Glossary

accommodate	to make room for
ambitious	having a desire to achieve a particular goal
amenities	something that provides convenience or enjoyment
attributed	explained by indicating a cause
cuisine	style of cooking
curriculum	the courses of study offered at an educational institution
dilemmas	problems involving difficult choices
enrollment	registration for a course
illiteracy	inability to read or write
indigenous	native to a place
interrelationships	relationships that have mutual connections
literate	able to read and write
mutual	shared
perpetuate	to cause something to last forever
prestigious	having a high reputation; honored
segment	separate piece of something
tuition	money paid for schooling
urban	having to do with a city
urbanized	caused to take on characteristics of someone or something from a city

Additional Resources

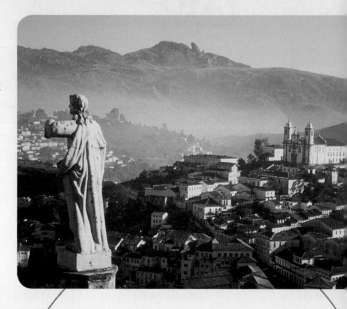

IN THE LIBRARY

Richard, Christopher, and Leslie Jermyn. *Brazil. 2nd Ed*. New York: Benchmark Books, 2002.

Greenbaum, Harry. *Brazil*. Philadelphia: Chelsea House Publishers, 2003.

Heinrichs, Ann. *Brazil*. New York: Children's Press, 2007.

Tahah, Raya. *The Yanomami of South America*. Minneapolis, Minn.: Lerner Publications Co., 2002.

Scoones, Simon. *Focus on Brazil*. Milwaukee, Wisc.: World Almanac Library, 2007.

Shields, Charles J. *Brazil*. Philadelphia, Pa.: Mason Crest Publishers, 2004.

ON THE WEB

For more information on this topic, use FactHound.
1. Go to *www.facthound.com*
2. Type in this book ID: 0756524423
3. Click on the *Fetch It* button.

FURTHER READING

Look for more Global Connections books.

Teens in Australia

Teens in China

Teens in France

Teens in India

Teens in Israel

Teens in Japan

Teens in Kenya

Teens in Mexico

Teens in Russia

Teens in Saudi Arabia

Teens in Spain

Teens in Venezuela

Teens in Vietnam

Source Notes

Page 33, column 1, line 12: Bruno Noronha. E-mail Interview by Shelly Lyons. 26 Oct. 2006.

Page 33, column 2, line 6: Ibid.

Page 71, column 2, line 5: Miriam Jordan. "For Some Young Brazilians, Skateboarding Jump-Starts Fame." *The Wall Street Journal*. 3 Nov. 2005. 5 Dec. 2006. www.post-gazette.com/pg/05307/600109.stm

Page 77, column 2, line 4: Bruno Noronha.

Pages 84–85, At a Glance: United States. Central Intelligence Agency. *The World Factbook—Brazil*. 30 Nov. 2006. 5 Dec. 2006. www.cia. gov/cia/publications/factbook/geos/br.html

Select Bibliography

Amazon Outreach. "The Short-term Missionary Handbook." *Dallas: Amazon Outreach*. 15 June 2006. www.amazonoutreach.org/tripprepmain.html

Ang, Eng Tie. "The Ultimate Feijoada Experience." *Brazzil Magazine* 14 May 2005. 6 Dec. 2006. www.brazzil.com/content/view/9245/0

Athan, Mattie Sue. *Complete Guide to the Companion Quaker Parrot.* Hauppauge, N.Y.: Barron's, 1997.

BBC News. "Amazon Drought Emergency Widens." 15 Oct. 2005. 5 June 2006. http://news.bbc.co.uk/2/hi/americas/4344310.stm

Brasil, Antonio. "Television in Brazil: Citizen Kane Revisited, or As the Globo Turns?" *Television Quarterly* 35 (Winter 2005). pp. 34–40.

"Brazil." *Worldatlas.com*. 15 June 2006. http://worldatlas. com/webimage/countrys/samerica/br.htm

Cook, Johanna M. *A Contemporary Analysis of Child Labor.* Marianist Social Justice Collaborative, Summer 2005.

Denes, Christian Andrew. "Bolsa Escola: Redefining Poverty and Development in Brazil." *International Education Journal* 4, no. 2 (2003), pp. 137–47.

Diogo Azevedo Lyra et al. *Rio Report: Police Violence and Public Insecurity*. Trans. Lincoln Ellis et al. Rio de Janeiro: Justiça Global, 2004.

"Discovery Atlas: Brazil Revealed." Peter Honors (producer). The Discovery Channel. Bethesda, Md. 15 Oct. 2006.

Inciardi, James A., and Hilary L. Surratt. "Children in the Streets of Brazil: Drug Use, Crime, Violence, and HIV Risks." *Substance Use and Misuse: 1997.*

Jordan, Miriam. "For Some Young Brazilians, Skateboarding Jump-Starts Fame." *The Wall Street Journal*, 3 Nov. 2005. 24 July 2006. www.post-gazette.com/ pg/05307/600109.stm

Maas, Helma. "Helping Brazilian Children Whose Lives Revolve Around Garbage Dumps." *UNICEF At a Glance: Brazil—Real Lives.* 18 June 2006. www.unicef.org/infobycountry/brazil_1920.html

Marques, Neusa Maria, and John Simons. *Motivational Determinants of Teenage Pregnancy in a Deprived Area of Recife, Brazil.* IUSSP General Population Conference, Salvador, Bahia, Brazil, Session S86: Young People's Reproductive Health, August 2001.

Rodrigues, Paulo. "A Glance at the Brazilian Pet Food and Supplies Market." 23 July 2003. U.S. & Foreign Commercial Service and U.S. Department of State, 2004. 18 May 2006. http://strategis.ic.gc.ca/epic/internet/inimr-ri.nsf/en/gr118346e.html

Somers, Marie-Andrée, Patrick J. McEwan, and J. Douglas Willms. "How Effective Are Private Schools in Latin America?" *Comparative Education Review* 48, no. 1 (2004), pp. 48–69.

Thompson, Sheila. "Cordel Literature." Maria-Brazil: Home of Brazilian Culture on the Web. 18 June 2006. www.maria-brazil.org/cordel.htm

Umayahara, Mami. "Regional Overview of Progress Toward EFA Since Dakar: Latin America." *Education for All Global Monitoring Report.* Executive Office, Education Sector UNESCO. 1 April 2005. 4 May 2006. http://unesdoc.unesco.org/images/0014/001462/146204e.pdf

"Latin America and the Caribbean: Brazil." United Nations Educational, Scientific and Cultural Organization. 14 June 2006. http://portal.unesco.org/geography/en/ev.php-URL_ID=2491&URL_DO=DO_TOPIC&URL_SECTION=201.html

United States Central Intelligence Agency. *World Factbook: Brazil.* 30 Nov. 2006. 7 Dec. 2006. www.cia.gov/cia/publications/factbook/geos/br.html

Index

About the Author
Caryn Gracey Jones

Caryn Gracey Jones is a freelance writer. She and her husband live in Denver, Colorado. Caryn worked in children's publishing, including at Compass Point Books for nearly five years. She has also worked in several nonprofit organizations, including the Children's Museum of Denver, March of Dimes of southeast Wisconsin, and Mile High United Way. She has a bachelor's degree in journalism from Marquette University and is working on her master's degree in writing from De Paul University.

About the Content Adviser
Jose Javier Lopez, Ph.D.

Our content adviser for *Teens in Brazil*, Dr. Jose Javier Lopez, is an associate professor in the Department of Geography at Minnesota State University, Mankato. He is an experienced middle school book reviewer, and his current research interests include social and economic geography and Latin America.

border to border · teen to teen · border to border · teen to teen · border to border